WHAT SHE WANTS

WHAT SHE WANTS

poems on

*Obsession, Desire,
Despair, Euphoria*

&

Kim Dower

*For Bill —
fellow poet
with
love*

Red Hen Press | *Pasadena, CA*

Book design by Mark E. Cull

Library of Congress Cataloging-in-Publication Data

Names: Dower, Kim, author.
Title: What she wants : poems on obsession, desire, despair, euphoria / Kim Dover.
Description: First edition. | Pasadena, CA: Red Hen Press, 2025.
Identifiers: LCCN 2024018859 (print) | LCCN 2024018860 (ebook) | ISBN 978-1-63628-263-3 (casebound) | 9781636282626 (trade paperback) | ISBN 9781636281551 (ebook)
Subjects: LCGFT: Poetry.
Classification: LCC PS3604.O9395 W47 2025 (print) | LCC PS3604.O9395 (ebook) | DDC 811/.6—dc23/eng/20240429
LC record available at https://lccn.loc.gov/2024018859
LC ebook record available at https://lccn.loc.gov/2024018860

The National Endowment for the Arts, the Los Angeles County Arts Commission, the Ahmanson Foundation, the Dwight Stuart Youth Fund, the Max Factor Family Foundation, the Pasadena Tournament of Roses Foundation, the Pasadena Arts & Culture Commission and the City of Pasadena Cultural Affairs Division, the City of Los Angeles Department of Cultural Affairs, the Audrey & Sydney Irmas Charitable Foundation, the Meta & George Rosenberg Foundation, the Albert and Elaine Borchard Foundation, the Adams Family Foundation, Amazon Literary Partnership, the Sam Francis Foundation, and the Mara W. Breech Foundation partially support Red Hen Press.

First Edition
Published by Red Hen Press
www.redhen.org

ACKNOWLEDGMENTS

Deepest gratitude and tremendous appreciation for Kate Gale, Mark E. Cull, and the dedicated, creative team of Red Hen Press.

Many thanks to the editors of the following journals and publications in which these poems first appeared:

Air Kissing on Mars (Red Hen Press, 2010): "Even in a Dream," "He Doesn't, She Does," "His Flavors Are Tender," "The Mole They Cut Out Of Your Chest," "She blew her nose," "She Is Awakened By A Hair," "Turbulence," "Waiting For You in the Bar"; *Beat Not Beat, An Anthology of California Poets Screwing on the Beat and Post-Beat Tradition* (Moon Tide Press, 2022): "Doing Nothing"; *Book of Matches*: "Ode to the Phone Booths in New York City," "Visiting Baudelaire"; *Interlitq*, "California Poets Pt. 5": "'You must be joking, I never eat breakfast.'"; *James Dickey Review*: "Doing Nothing"; *Last Train to the Missing Planet* (Red Hen Press, 2016): "Abandoned," "Candlelight Asylum," "Desire is the Fire," "A Fly with One Wing is Watching Me," "How I Learned to Love," "How to Celebrate the End of the World," "I Want to See You Glow," "Introspection," "Minor Tremors," "New Year's Eve," "Only You are You," "Punch Massage," "Reaching for the Moon," "She can't hear the things he says," "This Morning is For You," "What She Wants," "Years Later"; *Life and Legends*: "A Fly with One Wing is Watching Me"; *Los Angeles Review*: "How to Celebrate the End of the World," "Unruly Aura"; *Los Angeles Times*: "Doing Nothing"; *Plume*: "Promiscuous"; *San Diego Reader*: "What it Means When You Dream You Bought a Red Cadillac"; *Slice of Moon* (Red Hen Press, 2013): "Guilty Pleasures," "His Other Girlfriend," "It's Not That"; *Sunbathing on Tyrone Power's Grave* (Red Hen Press, 2019): "The Echo of Love," "Ink," "Love Hurts," "Risk," "Townies," "Unruly Aura," "What it Means When You Dream You Bought A Red Cadillac."

For Erica Jong
cherished poet, writer, mentor, friend
with admiration & love

In memory of
Stephen Dunn

To my Poetry Angel, without whom . . .

CONTENTS

INFATUATION

CRYSTALLIZATION

DETERIORATION

ECSTATIC RELEASE

"Our obsessions don't change; just the way we write about them."
—The author tells this to her students
but can't remember who said it.

"Poetry is not for personal confessions; it expresses another personality
that belongs to everyone."
—George Seferis

"When we love we are never free"
—Jill Bialosky

"All girls should have a poem
written for them even if
we have to turn this God-damn world
upside down to do it."
—Richard Brautigan

"Somewhere in history
Somewhere in untold ages
Somewhere in the sands of time
Somewhere in the vast seas of eternity
There is one person
Only one
Who could understand me and love me
And you're it
So get with it"
—Bill Knott

Limerence *noun*—the state of being obsessively infatuated with someone, usually accompanied by delusions of or a desire for an intense romantic relationship with that person: *Her limerence lasted for around three months before she actually met him.*

Today, many scientists and mental health professionals believe that **limerence is not only a psychological state but also a neurological one**, caused by low levels of the neurotransmitter serotonin in the brain.

Four Stages of Limerence

- Infatuation
- Crystallization
- Deterioration
- Ecstatic Release

"Never to have betrayed, admit it,
is a kind of lethargy or rectitude,
a failure, pure."

—Anonymous Poet

INFATUATION

She'll do anything for food,

the dog walker tells me.
She speaks quietly, not wanting
to insult her heavy-boned, one blue,
one brown-eyed beast tugging
at her leash. *We did a doggie
ancestor test,* she confides, *discovered
she's part wolf, part miniature poodle.*
Must be the poodle part makes her so
ravenous; small creatures are ruthless
feeders. Think of enraptured rats
gnawing their way through orange trees,
babies nursing—sucking so fiercely
they can burst a nipple. Think of your
heart, size of a throbbing fist, the part
of you that will do anything for love.

UNRULY AURA

The cashier at the health food store
tells me I have a beautiful aura.
Wait, I tell her, if you want to see
a really beautiful aura, wait until I've taken
my Renew Life, Ultimate Flora, Probiotic.
After that my aura will knock your socks off.
She smiles at me and rings me up. My money
has a beautiful aura, too. My dollar bills
float out of my pink wallet. The man behind me
swells from the heat I generate. Each step I take
brings me closer to God, the final, fabulous aura.
Take my hand, I tell her, squeeze my aura—
it's hungry, and looking for someone to devour.

THE BEAUTIFUL SHOULD-NOTS

She believes the men in her life,
like her physicians, should have
different roles: husband—primary
care-giver—while the specialists
treat those precious needs.
Be loyal, discreet, understand the gift
of a secret, she may love you.
Right now, the man she wants most
is the one offering thunderous afternoons.
She needs no man for salvation.
She's already unlocked the mysteries
of life. These mysteries are held tight
in the closed fists of the beautiful should-
nots that she continues to pry open.
It's what she does.

WHAT SHE WANTS

She wants to take the rocks
out of his pockets
be the puzzle
he keeps going back to
the clue
that solves it
she wants to be the sweat
on his neck
his holiday dinner
with two kinds of stuffing
the bandage across his chest
that stops the bleeding
the wax he drips
on his other
girlfriend's belly
the breeze
through his window
the butter he licks
from the corners
of his mouth
the only kiss
lingering on his lips
the milk in his coffee
the recurring dream
he waits for
book he gets lost in
kitten he rescues from the alley
she wants to be his last
meal before they flip

the switch and she wants to be
the one that pulls him
out of the chair
the shoes he wears
to escape
the song he sings
as they're running

KISSES WITH DREAMS IN THEM

After James M. Cain and Wallace Stevens

She told him she wanted kisses
with dreams in them,
the kind of kiss
you might only have once,
the kind of kiss upon which
your future
world depends

SHE TELLS HIM WHAT SHE THINKS
ABOUT BETRAYAL

It's useless to ban ourselves from feeling
love. Is it even possible? When someone
we love dies, don't we think of the others
who've gone before? Doesn't one love pour
into the stream of the others? She knows things.
She's not afraid to feel. Only the opposite.
What does it mean to want what we shouldn't have?
The quadruple bypass patient craves a double
cheeseburger with extra bacon, but he does not
feel guilty for wanting it. And if he knew
it wouldn't kill him, he'd be slurping one
right now in front us, his clothes loosened,
his fingers thick with ketchup.
The feeling desire gives, the endorphin popping
soul lifting, secret smile in our pocket fueling
the day cannot be something we shouldn't have.
No ketchup required! The only betrayal is to deny
the joy of the heart. If one is lucky enough
to have new feelings awakened, celebrate!
A secret life can make one's real life come alive
in surprising ways, can turn it, miraculously
into one's greatest secret.

HIS FLAVORS ARE TENDER

night time at a gelato cafe she sees him
is attracted by the way his hand
cradles the dish stirred by how he feeds
the sweetness into his mouth closing his eyes
with each spoonful
so distracted she barely touches
her Mexican vanilla mango pistachio melting fast
as she imagines him feeding her
she wants to be the plastic spoon he's licking
on both sides his shoulders twitching wants to be inside
the deep cup he's scraping on the bottom she thinks
his flavors are tender as her own lips
she longs to make out with him all night
their flavors mingling as she feeds him her body
one bite at a time

GET AN AFTERLIFE

She wants him like she used to want
a chocolate cream soda or a double
double cheese. Now it's only him she wants
to devour—his kisses—the ones that ignite
her bones, the kisses that will hunt her down
in the afterlife.

SHE IS AWAKENED BY A HAIR

She's awakened by a hair in her mouth.
It's not enough to kill her, no
that would take a locomotive crashing
through her window, a train way off track

thundering through her bedroom,
the moon on its back.
It's simply a hair
stuck to the roof of her mouth,

her tongue working to pry it loose.
Whose hair is it, anyway?
Is it the same dark hair she saw
floating in the bowl of vanilla gelato

she ate before bed?
Could it be this hair belonged
to that mechanic she once knew—
they made out on the carousel swan,

kissed till their lips bled—surely
a hair or two had been dislodged,
might have settled inside the cave
of her throat, only to resurface as a wish?

Is it possible the hair was placed
in her mouth by a higher power,
a mysterious donor, to remind her
that dreams are fleeting, even in sleep? No.

No. She realizes this is the same strand
she twisted around her tongue
one night when she was young,
sitting straight up in bed,

shadows from her closet
moving in beside her, as she slowly
closed the knot making a promise to herself
she still struggles to forget.

HIS TEETH MARKS
MAKE HER BEAUTIFUL

after he leaves
she see the imprints
on her belly
seashells, scorpions, half
moon embedded in her flesh
one wing out the door
destination unknown

REACHING FOR THE MOON

Tonight the moon will be so close
you can climb a tree, the tips
of your fingers will almost touch
its marbled face. Try to kiss
its luminescence as it floods you
with desire, anticipation consuming
your body as you swoon deeper
into yourself, a cat in heat craving
what is not beautiful. Stretch
for your moon, bigger than you've ever
imagined. You can no longer ignore
what compels you to reach for sadness.
Longing is what lifts you; only a lifetime
of sorrow will fill you with joy.

ODE TO THE PHONE BOOTHS
IN NEW YORK CITY

We'd cram ourselves in after school
one more, just one more, ok, you,
our shoulders crushed, groping like idiots,
cheeks smashed against the glass, one of us
with a finger in the accordion door,
pour our dimes into the slot
call our mothers to say Donna's for dinner
or Joey's to study then off we'd go
to Central Park. Sometimes it was just me
and Melissa, thunderstorms humidity
creeping into the booth, she'd sit on the seat,
heavy phone book on a wire swaying between us,
while I made collect calls with a fake credit card
to random people, the excitement killing us.
Senior year it'd be me alone, excusing myself
from my parents' dinner table, running a brush
through my hair, elevator down, making the call
to my boyfriend, filthy receiver tight in my hand,
mouthpiece caked with someone else's spit,
smelling like the inside of someone else's mouth,
I'd hang up if his mother or sister answered
they couldn't know we were about to meet,
walk into the dark opening of the park
find our spot below the American Elms
that lined the river, my heart pounding,
fingertips laced with the sweat of strangers.

NEAR THE END OF THE WORLD

She sees him from her window.
His is the only light still on
in the middle of a foggy night.
She's only up because she's afraid
to go back to sleep after awakening
from a dream where they carried her
naked body into a cave. She's shivering,
but the sight of him warms her.
She's felt his gaze before.
Tonight she lets him see
everything. She imagines this plague
making sense if they were alone
together, self-isolated, new.
He would give her the best part
of his heart, fill her with his secrets,
and she might show him what no one else
has ever bothered to want to know.
For them, what might happen near the end
of the world is an opening to another.
No fireworks in her cave. Just a pink
paper lantern that won't stay still,
that promises to blow up when desire
meets fulfillment and loneliness
is only a memory from that other world.

LOVE POEM

Just once before we crash
before we liquefy our passions
salty with years
from holding
someone else's heart
grinding our passions
into a wall
rush into me while I live
let me feel your heart
inside my chest
trust me to give
birth to you
see me
from the inside complete
the puzzle of being alive
just once flow and gather
before the storm
pushes us out to sea

REFRAIN

I stopped myself from seeing you today
But the lake looked clean and inviting
Kiss me goodbye and send me away
But the lake looked clean and inviting
I stopped myself from calling you tonight
But the lake looked clean and inviting
I told myself it's just not right
But the lake looked clean and inviting
I played the flute in junior high
But the lake looked clean and inviting
I once knew a man who said he could fly
But the lake looked clean and inviting
Come with me and I'll ruin your life
But the lake looked clean and inviting
But the lake
the lake looked clean
clean
and inviting

STUFF LIKE THAT

In the meantime,
he says, spread
your legs,
I want to disappear
in you, and stuff
like that.

She wants him
to disappear in her,
be overwhelmed by love
exploding
in her guts,

kisses too wild
to stay put on her lips,
kisses searching
for a permanent home.

She will spread
her legs
invite him
to disappear
so many
confused
kisses.

She will never confess
how one escaped
found refuge
inside her
where it lives

forever
hatching
baby kisses
by the second
and stuff
like that.

HE DOESN'T, SHE DOES

He doesn't want to think of her.
Can't risk her face showing up
in his sock drawer,

her butt filling his mind as
salad is served.
He doesn't want to remember

his face between her legs,
a word she whispered on the phone,
can't risk going to sleep imagining

holding her body tucked inside his,
her belly flat under his hand, his mouth
resting against her neck.

He can't think of her when she's not there
only in the moment when and where
they touch they know what might never be,

even then he doesn't want to look; but she
always seems to think of him,
in the shower, in the gym, feels him floating

under the covers while she's tight in bed,
turns into the pillow to crush her head.
She refuses to toss him out of her dreams,

her body aching because it seems
the chance to have him is deliciously slim.
He doesn't think of her; she thinks of him.

OBSESSION

She reads that a squirrel's
front teeth
never stop growing.
She will look into this.
She will set the record straight.

TO FILL EACH BLANK PAGE

From a man she had occasion to meet
on the subway, one black out

night headed for the Heights,
she was going Salsa Dancing

in someone else's clothes,
a wrap skirt easily

unwrapped, stilettos barely
holding her up: *posture is everything*

she could hear her mother say, and
don't think for a minute

she didn't love him, she did, he
held her elbow as they jumped

from the El, dropped
into the Hudson

like the half-eaten bride and groom
from the top of the wedding

cake, such a dark cold river moving
north, flowing both ways.

INTROSPECTION

I walk over to the full-length
mirror, take off my robe
look at my body as if I were you

looking at me, touch my breasts
drop my hand to my belly
rub and pinch as if my fingers

were yours, watch you
watch me like I'm in a play
and you're my only audience.

We're not alone.
The young girl inside me
is standing on her bed

watching her shape take form
her eyes lowered but anxious
for you to see. The pregnant me

she's here too—see how tightly
her skin is stretched
over her belly, her insides

riding her like a cannonball of waves.
Look at the scar on my left
shoulder. Have you ever noticed

that before? I need you to know
my body's whole story,
from the fever when I was born

when they lowered me
into a mixing bowl of ice
to when the bleeding began

I doubled over, no one
was there, no one can ever
really be there

can they? Even our toes change
shape in the dark.
I'm ready to be turned inside out.

WARNINGS

This Plastic Bag is Not a Toy
Do Not Remove This Tag
No not Swallow or Inhale
Discontinue Use if Rash Appears

Despite these warnings
I dress my bag up
like a doll
take her on errands
lick shampoo off my fingers
inhale the orange scented
floor wax
I tempt my rashes
with more rashes
until my body screams
for more

Give me a *real* warning:
Dirty needles
Cross at the Intersection
Tsunami Risk
Don't succumb
to that first crazy kiss

VISITING BAUDELAIRE

Walking miles through ancient
air, skinny streets, my head filled
with his clouds like a tic fills itself
with blood. I butter my baguette,
length of a baton, as I stroll to his grave.
Everyone has given me pre-trip
tourist tips: where to go, what to see,
every friend who's been seduced by Paris,
as if we're all in love with the same woman,
arguing over what's her best part,
how long did she invite us to stay
deep inside. I'm here for a week,
my goal to visit Baudelaire's grave
and finally I've arrived but with nothing
to give except an unfinished poem
which I place beside the dried
yellow roses, discolored pack of Gauloises,
another visitor's engraved leather notebook.
There's no place for me to sit and talk with him.
The sun burns a hole through his magnificent
clouds, even though he's dead I'm too shy
to tell him how I feel.

WHO'S TO SAY

every bird I see
doesn't speak
only to me
Who's to say
the kiss I feel
in the wind
isn't sent by you
Who's to say
you're not the moon
in my pocket?

PLAGUE INFIDEL

She has always believed in what feels
good. Feeling good is what keeps her
going. So now, she imagines this man
entering her cave. She would hand him her
golden flashlight so he could see every
crack. The cave is a secret, like her bath
used to be, when she'd undress, step
into the tub for a guest she wanted
to know better. She wants to know this man
better, although she believes she already
knows him. She's not without morals.
She has plenty. But she cannot help herself.
Her body has always been her go to place,
not only for herself, for those who are unlucky
enough to ignite the spark that shoots up her
adventurous spine. Normal desires?
She doesn't know what those are.
Her desires simmer even when she's desperate
to blow them out. Even when she knows
the new world she's opening could crumble
like a house in the Big One—chimney coming
down first—brick by brick, and even then
she will throw off her clothes and dance
in the rubble.

DESIRE IS THE FIRE

It isn't always what you have
Fills your life with pleasure
Often what you wish was yours
Becomes your secret treasure

SHE TELLS HIM,

squeeze me
music will come out
she tells him this
because she wants
to impress him
wants him to believe
if he squeezes her
music will come out
so he does
when he does
a tune flows
from her belly
smoky, guttural
a tune he remembers
for the rest of the day
she wants the sounds
her body makes
to haunt him
she doesn't know
how hard he will squeeze
the next time
if his squeeze
might kill her song
even before
it begins to play

IMPOSSIBLE

He can't want
what he knows
she can give
and she can't want
to give it.

CRYSTALLIZATION

LOVE

"Everything was beautiful and nothing hurt."
—Kurt Vonnegut, *Slaughterhouse-Five*

nothing between us
but the moments
before we kiss
when we enter
the deep forest
of ourselves
where everything
grows wild
birds sip nectar
from one another's beaks
pounding electric joy
through the night
his face
hers to memorize
her body
his to explore
they would fall hard
because
when she smiled at him
he was finally home

THIS MORNING ON
THE WET GATE

a flower and a fly
what were they doing
before I interrupted them?

WILDERNESS KISSES

our kisses are trails
leading me through the forest of you
fragrant electric wet
with secrets
deep in the woods of one another
let me stay lost let me never find
my twisted way home

OBLIVION

me and you we
wait for the train
hear its chesty cough
hammer the tracks
jump back
as it thunders by
its force
glistening metal
drains our faces
like our kiss
rendering our lips
numb
the screech
of love

I Want to See You Glow,

he tells me, so I rub pet products
over my body, oil to make a dog's coat
glossy. The hair on my arms is sparse,
but I run fast and have an appetite
like a Weimaraner. I want to feel
as good to the touch as a dog
after a day in a dog spa, as energetic,
intelligent, alert, steady. This human
life is not right anymore. Look around.
Join me for a chew treat and a dish of water.

WHAT IT MEANS WHEN YOU DREAM
YOU BOUGHT A RED CADILLAC

it means your face is on fire
it means your hands grab anything that moves
it means you want to be kissing her scarlet knees
it means you want one bloody shrieking crimson haunted wish
to finally come true as you speed past
your blindfolded childhood   drive until your life
finally works   it means you want a ride so fast so smooth you'll glide
into home right through your front door no questions asked
it means your inflamed dream is racing you into the future
where naked people are waiting to greet you embrace you
are lined up to jump inside the passenger seat
it means your headache will recede into a night of fingertips
easing the pain your back drenched against the leather
cherry colored ignition blush like your first hot wheeled crush
energy pulsing feet solid on the pedal touch
your hands 10 and 2 o'clock like they taught you back then when
all you cared about was her skirt riding up over your cool hand
slap her thigh it hurt to look her in the eye one kiss to last all summer

RISK

no one's ever stolen
the moon for me
hoisted it out of the sky

carried it on his back
rolled it across his shoulders
its cold white fumes

blasting him through space
stars sprawled out like clues
under his feet oh no one's

ever dared steal the moon for me
until you who sifted through
dirty clouds flew faster higher

than the hungry birds gnawing
the air their wings askew
believing the moon was theirs

THIS MORNING IS FOR YOU

This morning is for you
sideways bird not quite awake

not ready to make
sounds that will astonish.

This morning's for you
fading stars still tucked

into the bleary sky
your final twinkle vibrating

the heavens before dawn
kills you off.

This morning is for the bruise
that lingers on my arm

purple as a groggy sunset
reminding me I can take

any punch that comes my way
silently charged as twilight

fearless as the night
fearless as I for loving you

completely as I do, surrendering
to light, black into blue,

this morning's a buried treasure
this morning is for you.

PUNCH MASSAGE

This is what they do
to relieve the pain.

Stay still, he says, as he thrusts
his fist into her belly

turning the color of a child's
cocktail, not quite pink,

rosy as her cheek
when fever would spike.

Don't move, he says, as he jabs
his knuckles into her gut.

She keeps her eyes open,
do it harder, she whispers,

her voice hoarse with
expectations, he delivers

his face, neck coated with sweat
another fast one in her sweet spot

where they cut the cord
when she was born,

the core from where she needs
to be released once more

so she can enter his rage
pavilion, live inside his anger,

disappear in the glow, the power
of his hands. He wants to be sure

she can take all he's got to give,
hopes she asks him for more.

This is how they create. This is how
they know who they are.

ONLY YOU ARE YOU

The way your lips curve
into a halfway smile
like the joke's not ready

you save the punch
line for dark.
Only you are the tiger

in my recurring dream
giant cat I taunt, run from.
Only you are the one I speak to

when I'm not speaking
blanket that covers me
wraps me tight until dawn

as you hike the shadowed hills,
moon stepping back just for you
only you, offering a fresh sky.

I'll never know where you go,
wish I could rescue you
make us real make us right,

woo you from the cave
where your heart hides you,
bare, unfed, not able to dig

into the lighthouse of bones
we both crave to suck dry.
I sleep inside your mouth,

echo of your voice vibrates
like music from a party
in a faraway room;

can you hear it, too, only you?

INK

I unscrew my fountain pen
a gift from a writer I
love—that deep ink kind of love
that can never be erased.
He tells me I need to remove
the cartridge before I board
the plane, tells me it will explode
if it remains locked in the pen,
like my heart sometimes feels
it's going to explode so confined
in my chest. This scares me, you see
because I'm not sure how to replace
the cartridge without breaking
the pen and I don't want to fuck
it up. I will try as hard as I can
to follow instructions and not
push too hard; I will try to un-
screw and re-screw and it should
all be fine. After all, it's just a pen,
albeit a pen that when I hold
in my hand it appears my hand
is dancing the words right onto the page,
the words circling back into my heart,
my heart pounding to get out.

HE DOESN'T KNOW

so many things
he doesn't know

like how his kisses
silence the voices

in her head
quiet as snow falling

on ancient trees
or the way his hands

can soothe the ears
of a crocodile

GUILTY PLEASURES

My boyfriend tells me, *put a candy*
on your naked belly, take a picture,
send it to me. I'm far away from LA,
Helmsley Park Lane Hotel, silent on the 37th
floor, white curtains opened, picture window
big as a Broadway stage. Lights, not the moon
command the night. I watch them rule,
slowly turn off, as the buildings grow invisible,
disappear into the steel sky. I spot a rooftop way below
bathed in floodlights, two chaise lounges, a table, plants,
but where's the couple that should be making love
in the chilly October air? Why is there so much
candy in hotel rooms all laid out like a concession stand,
right there on the dresser, easy reach, take what you want,
as much as you want, even if you don't want it at all,
not realizing it'll cost you maybe $5.00 for a Snickers bar,
who knows how much for Kit Kats since they come double,
even if you take a nibble, or just one Skittle, they'll charge you:
open the wrapper, it's yours. Who really even *wants*
candy at night? I'm searching for life inside the blackness of night,
watch the colors of stained glass radiate from the top of the Chrysler Building
which appears to be floating in air. At one time, but only for eleven months,
it was the tallest building in New York, until the Empire State Building
took its place. When the Twin Towers were built, it was number three;
when the Towers came down, number two again. *Take a picture.*
I think about that Snickers on the dresser. Not that I really
want it, but because it's there I think I should have it,
because it's so quiet, I think I should keep myself awake.
I lie on the bed, place a chocolate covered almond on my naked belly,

feel the party coming on. *Send it to me.* Suddenly it's in my mouth, another, wrappers flying, I'm having a dark chocolate fever dream as American flags below wave the night inside out.

IF THAT'S WHAT YOU WANT

My body will form an S
Slide down a metal pole
If that's what you want

My heart will burn like coal
Stay hot for you all night
If that's what you want

My hands will hold you steady
Until the shaking stops
My eyes will transform you

Into an Island God
If that's what you want
If that's what you want

You can have it now
I will show you how
I will pull the knife

From your chest
So you can finally rest
Take it from me now.

LOVE HURTS

You are my tourniquet my Saturday
matinee, my jelly bean storm, pointer
and thumb you are my hidden door my home
is your skin you are the dream I taste the
moment I awake the bruised crime I live
to commit my drawbridge thunder shudder
you are my pink cloth childhood coat with
the velvet collar the red mark on my
arm the tunnel I crawl through on my hands
and knees the flapping bird struggling to fly

THE MOLE THEY CUT OUT OF YOUR CHEST

Where is it now?
Deep, you told me, they had to dig
through the heat to carve it out
this mole, an annoying imperfection

you wanted to be rid of.
Where is it now?
Did they name it before drowning it
in a saline filled test tube, or

did your mole escape?
Could it be traveling through space—
an eye craving new skin to grace,
hoping to land on the inner thigh

of a goddess or the cheekbone
of the girl you once loved?
I always noticed it, was attracted by the way
it glistened, brown, well-defined,

attentive on your smooth chest—
stood out like a special moment,
a warning, a button I might push
to let me inside.

Not having had the chance to say goodbye
I feel sad, missing the spot
that followed me as you'd slide
in and out looking into my eyes

the only flaw on your perfect skin.
Where is it now, the mole they cut out of your chest?
If it gets in touch, please tell it to come
languish behind my ear, ride high

on my shoulder praying to the sun,
or roll on my index finger
waiting for me to blow it away
into the Santa Ana winds.

WAITING FOR YOU IN THE BAR

I'm here you're
here, but we're here
separately, you in the room
flooded with smoke and sun

me in the lounge dark leather
seats surrounded by darker light.
I think you're not coming
forgot or got stuck in the endless

traffic we now call home.
I drink a tall vodka, suck the straw,
my only chance to survive,
get it deep inside, shut down the thought

you might not be arriving.
I know you're here, can feel you,
you're never late,
you don't forget, but I can't get

myself to look around, rather
drink another, imagine strolling
onto the beach, tide rolling out
wandering into someone else's dream,

a kiss floating onto my lips, maybe
yours? A white bird hovering
sending signals from a forgotten planet
calling me into another life.

I'm here, you're here, but it doesn't matter:
we've already been there and gone,
the moon following until it's ready
to pull us back.

FALLING IN LOVE TWICE

she didn't know she could learn
from a man who for so long
she could barely look at

without her insides dropping,
a man she'd think about
in the middle of the night

every night pull every hair
out of her body until her skin
cold and bare would forget

what it felt like to be held
she didn't know that time
would go by and she'd be able

to look him in the eyes, listen
to his words, let them in
like she'd let him into her fantasies

so many years before
desire cracked open lust's
surprise of still wanting him

DETERIORATION

SHEDDING

Don't make love to a married man
in his house there's too much evidence
you'll need to destroy—dripping on the white
linen couch, for example, could be the deal
breaker for future visits, certainly those long
dark hairs that will inevitably fall out in clumps
after embracing in the heat of lust, hair you brushed
seconds before you knocked on his door, hair
you'll watch him scoop off the floor with his hands
scan the pillow for more when moments ago
you lay swooning. You'll watch as he lifts
each strand like contraband. Your heart will drop
as he spots another, lunges to peel that slithering
snake off the pristine fabric. You'll understand why
this must be done, won't blame him for needing to cover
his tracks. He won't be aware of his zeal each time
he discovers another, won't know how badly this hurts you.
You're ashamed you even *have* hair, dumbfounded
by how it's coming undone in horrifying globs,
you're a *shedder*, improperly brushed, and you notice
he's not even keeping a lock to put in his drawer—
you're a criminal worshipping in the darkness of your love.
We take this risk because we can't help who we fall for,
want to breathe the air they breathe while waiting
for their coffee to drip, see the view they see at breakfast,
leave the imprint of our souls on their hardwood floors.
You'll get down on your knees, help him collect and discard
what comes from your body, knowing it belongs to him
even though he's throwing it away.

FORECAST

disturbance
will create
clouds so low
they will kiss
the roof
of your house
try to reach
inside them
grab a handful
of mist
each gray
lazy
drop
carries
a message
be lulled
by the song
inside fog
so thick
you won't see
the clear notes
that will lift you
into tomorrow's
sunshine
extended outlook:
heat lightning
too far away
to hear the breath
of thunder

CONTROL

There is eating and there is not eating.
I have done both. I have gorged on tri-colored
vegetable chips until salt oozed from my pores,
and my skin turned the color of a bruised
blue potato. I have denied myself all three meals,
fasted for days. I relate to dogs who fixate
on their owner's pockets waiting for treats
they know are buried. I don't have an eating disorder—
it's just my way of controlling my life. Denial
is its own reward. I keep my running shoes close,
my fanny pack loaded. I want to be ready for the big race.
They will call on me soon. They will call on all of us.
I want an empty stomach when I hear my name.
I want to be the fastest both in and out of love.

DRINKING COFFEE NAKED

What good is drinking coffee naked
when you're not here to watch?
Best to keep my clothes on
and stop dreaming! That first sip
of morning Joe, eyes closed,
memories pouring through me—
the swan in the hotel wading pool,
kissing under the noisy sheets—
first cup and for a few minutes
I'm the creator of my own life.
Thank Josephus Daniels,
Secretary of the Navy in 1913
for prohibiting alcohol aboard ships,
and giving coffee that cute nickname.
If not for him I might be sipping a smooth
Scotch on crushed ice with my deviled
eggs. Now there's a drink to have naked.

HIS OTHER GIRLFRIEND

"My *other* girlfriend lets me," he says while trying to stick it in
without lube. I don't care what his other girlfriend lets him do
or if she wears red satin dresses that slip off her shoulders,
has golden hair, can recite *The Wasteland* without stumbling,
I will show you fear in a handful of dust, is a landscape architect
who handpicks bricks that separate gravel from vegetables,
designs wagon wheels filled with purple and pink roses,
can drink an entire pitcher of beer in one gulp without burping,
writes in Japanese while humming the theme from *The Third Man.*
"My other girlfriend has her *own* girlfriend," he tells me, "they tiptoe
up my back, dive from my head to the couch." Why does he have to
tell me about his *other* girlfriend—me who can recite all the dialogue
from *High Plains Drifter* while walking on my window ledge,
twelve stories high, still believing there are reasons not to cry,
me who wades into the roughest ocean, puts my head below the surf,
swallows mouthfuls of fish that float down my throat, swim out my ass.
I've been cross-country skiing my way into his heart for years,
and the moonlight on the snow is beginning to fade.

PROMISCUOUS

Promiscuous is what my mother
called a friend of mine in high school.
It wasn't just the word, but the way
she said it—savoring every syllable
as if sipping a smooth single malt scotch.
Pro-mi-scu-ous, she would say—the way
she drops one boy for the next,
the way she dresses. I would admonish
myself—Why tell her *anything,* I'd rant
in my head, you stupid you.
My friend wore short dresses with boots,
left her legs bare, strong. I tried it once
but kept pulling my tights back on,
I was no slut like Marion. She was
probably sleeping with our English
teacher, Mr. Hardy, taught us *Madame
Bovary* and had dimples. Yes, for sure
she was sleeping with him, with her good
vocabulary and her bare legs.
Mr. Hardy used the word "promiscuous"
when teaching the story of Emma's compulsive
love for Rodolphe. The Cliffs Notes say
"she falls for him because of his stylish green
coat and his title, and he desires her because
she seems like an easy conquest." See:
promiscuity! Was Mr. Hardy Marion's
Rodolphe? I never had her over again,
after my mother's remark. I kept things
secret—those bare-legged things, as I pinched

my nipples to make them pop under my shirt,
meticulously drew the black liner under
my lids, as I rolled my tights off in the girl's
bathroom before I slid into the seat of my
11th grade math class, I too, would get a green
coated man! Perhaps Mr. Bander. After all,
I needed extra help in Geometry, not in language
or matters of the heart. I already knew then
what I know now. In short, it's no mystery
how sluts get to be sluts. It's all
knot in your stomach, headlong, obsession
and remorse, sizzle and ghost.

SHE CAN'T HEAR THE THINGS HE SAYS,

yet she listens anyway
knowing his words will cut her
like shards of glass from a flask

in which she'd like to mix him
a special cocktail.

She no longer feels sick
when his rants slice her in half
chooses to believe

he doesn't realize what he's saying,
how it sounds.

He'd better not touch her,
better not reach across the 400 thread count
pima cotton rose colored sheets crisscrossed
with blush stripes—*subtle* he said

when she brought them home,
they blend into the fabric, fade into the pattern
like a frightened child fades into the back

of her closet,
hides from the screamers

protected by darkness, holds her own hand.

They can't get me here, she thinks,

but here she is again,
grown up, in the back of a different closet,

the threads of ribbon laced around her soul
have come undone,

float above her, hover
as she humps the couch,
dances naked
toes pointing north,

she's powering through the tunnel of un-love,
gathering the strong ones still alive inside her,
will never return to the closet

for that's where
she keeps the bones,

the ones she's spent her life

sucking clean.

TURBULENCE

The pilot announces
the air will be choppy.

I turn to the clouds
scattered like a pattern on sheets

we'll never sleep on.
I think of your body

pressing me into the hotel bed,
your grip exquisitely tight

around my neck.
I lean my head against the hard

airplane window to feel the sun
pull me home

as we bump through unstable air,
rocky as a double life.

I pull the seat belt tight,
search for markings of life below

lakes, forests, baseballs rolling
in backyards too far down to see.

I memorize the sleeping faces
of passengers nearby, all of us

up in the air like the way I feel
each time we part.

The lives we're flying over,
the strangers by our sides

are as unknown as the ones we'll find
once we get back home.

She blew her nose

into a fresh pink tee shirt
plucked from her bottom
drawer. It's not that she didn't

have a tissue. She did.
The box on her bedside table
was well within reach

but she preferred the comfort
of cotton, of what she'd worn
the day before

things fell apart. It's safer to cry
into a tissue that can be flushed
in the toilet where she'd

vomited after listening to him
confess, pesto pasta from lunch
fighting its way back up.

She cried until a blue bird
flew out of her body,
the breeze from its wings

making her sneeze.
She blew her nose
into a fresh pink tee shirt

then used it to clean
the things on his bedside
table, rub the alarm

out of his clock, shine
the oval mirror as she watched
her face disappear.

NEW YEAR'S EVE

Wash your hands clean enough
to tackle the dip without a cracker.
Cleanse them of all past sins—those
you know you've committed as well as
the ones you only wish were yours.
Forget the foot rub you didn't really want
to give. Forget the stranger in the elevator.
Tonight our red dresses hug our bellies,
glitter is in our hair, gift-wrapping
sticks to our shoes, our shoes stick
to the floors of other people's kitchens.
Ranch dressing, everything fried, cold air
packing us inside, we say goodbye
to a year that slid under the door like
an unopened utility bill. The bedroom fills
with coats over coats stacked on the bed—
car keys, weed spilling out of pockets, tufted
bedspread covered by handbags, scarves,
dog hair, slipper sock, you on top
your hands on my throat pressing just
hard enough to get me to mean it when I say,
Happy New Year, lint ghosts trapped below
raising a toast, as we drift into
the demanding silence of January.

HOW I LEARNED TO LOVE

By trusting the moon even when I couldn't see it
By watching my cat lick between her claws

By watching them kiss in *Splendor in the Grass*
I leaned over the couch so I could see up close
No space between them so their love
Could not escape

I learned to love by feeling bad, feeling shame
I never meant to leave the milk out
I should have been the one to blame

I learned to love by protecting everyone but me
A spider edging along the windowsill

MINOR TREMORS

Family photos slanted
on the wall
must have shifted
after a small quake
I never felt
the impact of
I only remember that big one
shaking us awake at 4 a.m.
the two of us
trying to balance our way
along rippling floorboards
palms flat against the wall
our bodies hurled
down the long hall
struggling against the obscene
force of earth
to retrieve our son
sleeping in his crib

Can't put my finger on
the years
of minor tremors
between then and now
but I know things have changed
When did the cup on the top shelf
topple to its side
when did the hairline
fracture on the living room wall
become a crack spreading across the ceiling

When did I feel the shift
in my heart
They say the small ones
relieve the pressure
so the big one won't come
Still, every time I feel a truck
rumble through the alley
I brace myself
for the ground to finally open
I'm ready to slip away
into its burning core

IT'S NOT THAT

Every day I tap on the skull
of another dilemma:
which part of my heart

will I extinguish
which thought will I murder
what lie must I tell?

It's not that
you weren't once everything
I thought I wanted

it's just that I'm done
trying to pump milk
out of someone else's soul

get underneath another's body
squeeze their juice
into my parched mouth

It's not that
you haven't given me everything
you had to give

it's not that I didn't take it
a starved cat pouncing
from one shoulder to the other

it's not that
the pebbles in my throat
keep me from swallowing

it's that however near
or far away
I can still hear

you breathe
though I can no longer feel
the beating of your heart

EVEN IN A DREAM

Ray Ronci tried to murder me came after me
with a gun seriously I haven't seen him for 30 years
we parted friends but there he was
telling me he was going to kill me drove over
in a Honda with two friends all pale him
so serious I escaped but he came back later his
small black gun covered by a tissue
like that would hide it I saw it put my hand
over the hole like that would stop the bullet
like I could stop the days or the leaves from
slipping down the drain pipe falling as fast as
Ray Ronci's hair I could see even with his gun
even in a dream that he'd lost hair
did he see my eyes were not as clear
as they once were it was Saturday when I had the dream
two more days had fallen he didn't shoot me
but his beard was ashen as he took me to my bed
where we lay together in silence
as the phone kept ringing

THE ECHO OF LOVE

They send me to the hospital
for an echocardiogram so they can see
inside my heart. Lou, the technician

tells me the heart is like a house
with many rooms and this will show them
the size of the rooms

if they have cracks in the ceiling, leaks
in the pipes, a damaged sun porch. I can hear
whooshing, see my blood flow

see it drop, the colors on the screen,
red, blue, green like a geyser exploding,
like the colors of falling in love, blasting

through my body, flutter through the day,
same pounding, racing away,
my heart screaming let me out of here.

I say, Lou, how are things looking, pretty good,
huh? big flow all those colors, and he says,
we need to take a deeper look before we know

if there's a problem. I understand. Look as deep
as you need, Lou. You will be the only one
who'll ever know what goes on inside those chambers.

DISAPPOINTMENT

wraps around
her shoulders
like a cheap
scarf, spreads
like a rash
by evening
her chest a full glow
of angry bumps
itchy, relentless
now her legs
are covered too
raised red blotches
breathing, not possible
she is consumed
by Disappointment
tries to understand
what happened
how she might have
done things differently
Expectations:
the home wreckers
the enemy, the utensils
we use to keep the wound
from closing

Dr. Rosen Can Change Your Life in One Day,

my friend tells me as we ride the bus
down to 48th and Broadway—*he'll release
energy you've been holding onto for decades.*
I'm game. I'm wearing jeans, no underwear.
I want Dr. Rosen to know I've already released
a ton of energy, some of it in his waiting room,
and what I have left I want him to capture, trap
in a hatbox, donate to people who no longer care
if they can't find their keys, who've forgotten
the combination to their locks, people too tired
to roll over in bed and whisper I love you.

EVEN LUST

Steven meets him at my party,
thinks he's cute, pumps me—
do I know who's he been with before,

is that his *real* hair color? What about
those loafers? Is he single, sane, spooner?
Would he make him forget every bad

encounter he's ever had like that slob
who ghosted him or the urgent kisser?
Would he take him to that ecstatic place

he's only read about on tantric blogs?
Steven has the bluest eyes and when he smiles
a bright sun bursts through his heart.

I hope this guy is single and sane.
Not sure about spooner. For me, personally,
the heat of someone's breath on the back of my neck

while I'm trying to fall asleep is a red flag—
the kind of intimacy for which not even lust
has the energy to get dressed up for.

SHE NEVER SAID, *Don't Go*

She tried to discretely disappear out of love
leave no mark on herself, like a sunset
obscured by fog barely streaks the milky sky,
wanted to leave him thinking maybe
she still cared, test his own desire.
She never said, *don't* go, but not saying *stay*
was enough for him to leave. It was that easy.
You see he wanted to be forced, wanted her
to trace his finger down the scar on her chest.

IT WILL BE A SMALL THING

that puts you over the edge.
A bottle of water spills
on a pile of bills, you slam
the refrigerator shut, knock the milk
over on the beef you've been marinating.
You'll cry out the most horrible obscenities
strung together like the pearls
your mother gave you right before she died,
the ones you lost at that dingy hotel
where you never should have been,
the name of which you can't even remember.

TISSUE BOXES

She finds the extra tissue boxes
in the cabinet with the spices.
That's not where they should be,
she thinks, worried now
what else has been misplaced.

Where did he put the hair dryer,
for example, that belongs under
the sink, near the cotton balls
and peroxide? She's afraid she'll find it
in the drawer with the spatulas

or laying on top of the filthy
dust pan inside the musty vacuum closet.
So many things are getting misplaced.
She couldn't find the feta cheese—
might they be out of it?

So many thing are missing—
the laughter around the piano, the jokes
while dinner is served, the hot fudge
melting the vanilla, her smile at the end
of a long day of finding things in their places.

WAIT ON THE SIDE OF THE ROAD

she's coming back to get you
so just wait there
don't take a ride

with strangers
the flat blue sky
impossible to be true

she might be back to get you
she won't forget you but she's busy
right now she needs

to not be with you as she
travels the earth
in her multi-colored roadster

she has things she must do
can't be with you
the locket she wears

chokes her neck, cradles
your image in the depths
of her throat, the photo torn

in the corner from where she ripped
it apart that morning she finally knew
& now it's her turn to shine

a light down into her heart
plead with herself to not
repeat the crime

HOW TO CELEBRATE THE END OF THE WORLD

Undress.
Take everything off. Everything.
Rub your nipples with grape-seed oil.
Sit up straight in your most uncomfortable chair.
Remind yourself of all the good things you've done.
Have you done anything good?
Tell me what you've done.
Have you given birth to a child
Who danced around the house wearing ninja clothes?
Did you visit your dying mother every last day until
The day she died whispering thank you inside your moist hands?
Be quiet.
Don't look me in the eyes. Look down.
Have you cooked meals for the homeless?
Sat with them while they ate?
Have you ever rescued anyone?
Tell me the good things you've done.
Then remember the times you lost yourself in sorrow.
Waded in pools of it, banged your head against the ledge,
Hated yourself for wanting love, or showing how you felt.
Remember the moments it hurt so bad you had to pull out
Just in time. Let's prepare together for the end of the world.
Forget what I previously said. Let's dress. Let's layer ourselves
With color, texture, linen and cashmere, beads in our hair, smear
Our blood on one another's faces. Stretch ourselves
Into eternity, breathe life into whatever dream we've been keeping
Under wraps, jump the fence together, melt the line with heat
From our kisses, obliterate it with desire, cross over
Into the end of the world, the beginning of another, locked
In an emergency embrace.

TWO WEEKS LATER

Home. Heartsick. When she touches
herself in the shower, it's his hand
she imagines. How can this happen,
she whispers into the mirror, why
does it hurt so much? Why did we come
together only to be in so much pain
when we separate? It's what the living
do, she thinks. She will live off the memory
of his smile, the memory of the way it felt
when he slid inside her, her body reaching
to meet him. She will have a thin slice
of chocolate layer cake night after night,
put a bite in her mouth, let it melt, eyes closed,
tell herself, yes, this cake tastes as good
as it looks. And what will she do now?
How does one stretch a memory wide enough
to cover up a life?

ECSTATIC RELEASE

SHHH

our secret
will die with me

I will swallow it
as I take

my last breath
feel it slide

like a block of ice
down my throat

into my hot belly
where it will dissolve

like my heart
we should have told

one other person
how we unlocked

the night air
like jasmine

how our scent
kept us alive

TOWNIES

don't talk
as much as city boys
their arms are bigger
they can drive a stick
they don't care
about restaurants
or perfume
they like to do it
all the time
anywhere
they have things
they keep
in boxes, like old snake
skins or buttons
from swap meets
I loved one once
he liked to do it
in my parents'
summer cottage
when they were out
getting vegetables
he'd scoop me up
like a fireman saving
my life, toss me
on the calico print couch
damp with salt air
my ass burned
from rubbing

against the coarse fabric
he gave me a hickey
the size of a heart
I watched it fade
like the sunset
as I took the ferry
back home

YEARS LATER,

sitting in my backyard
relieved to be feeling whole
with only a breeze for conversation
I think about you and how you loved
water sports, diving into the murky lake
while I'd hang on the beach zipped up
in a life preserver, promising I might
go on the boat for a quick ride around the edge
of the shore. I asked you to never turn on
the motor when I was aboard, *I like to take it slow,*
I told you, *take in the scenery.*
Once you brought a picnic:
lopsided sandwiches, meat half off,
not sure where you found the bread
but I forced mine down with a gulp
of Pabst (made your nuts cousin buy it for us),
iced cold and tasting nasty.
I would have done anything with you
back then, when the moon was watching
only us, your golden eyes, superhero
shoulders, would have split my life in two
with the paddle from your canoe would have
let you cut me deepest, but what was the use?
I was a summer visitor in your yearround world
too young to know why it was okay.
Your hair smelled of cedar, was held back
with a clip belonging to your winter girlfriend.
You were mine for July and I was terrified
of the shortness of the ride.

NEW LIFE

Take my breath
out of my chest
float it in the air
pick me up
so I can reach
for my own life
hold me like yours
would end if you
let me drop
then drop me
from the cliff
watch me fall
out of your arms
you think it's over
until you see clouds
pour from my heart
a storm retreating
into the sea

LONGING

I saw *Amour* last night, French film
about an old couple, "life, death,
and everything in between."
"Bring tissues," said a review,
but no tears came.
I still wonder this morning
why didn't I cry—what's wrong with me?
I hear the birds singing outside my window,
trapeze artists twirling their tiny bodies
from one branch to the next.
Pigeons are heavy, seem stupid, clueless,
not like these air magicians on my lemon tree.
A pigeon was in the movie,
flew in from the balcony onto the kitchen floor,
walked around pecking crumbs off the tiles.
The old man captured it in a blanket,
held it on his lap.
This upset me more than you can know.
My therapist has the sounds of chirping birds
piped into his waiting room.
For the first few sessions I thought the birds were real,
comforted knowing sparrows were perched close by
while I waited to be engorged with self-understanding.
When I found out the birds were fake
the whole idea of therapy lost its charm,
but I tried to rationalize: isn't it the same
as when they play a recording of ocean waves
during a massage? After all, the *sounds* are real,

they've just been captured, saved for moments
we crave their music. Like longing. The stab
of *desire* is real so we place it in a blanket,
hold it in our laps, feel its pulse throb in our fingertips,
as a flood of memories carries us into another body.

FIRST KISS

Manny the MRI technician hands me earplugs.
These will help, but won't eliminate the banging.
He gives me a tiny sedative to place under my tongue,
slides me into the dark tube, suggests I close my eyes,
think about nice things: glass of rosé, my first kiss.
I want to follow his instructions but my first kiss
with the dark-haired boy with fat lips, no good
at archery, Camp Trywoodie, was a bust.
Racket begins. I try to imagine what they might find.
Perhaps in my cerebellum, a family of idiots
playing Go Fish, discarded toys, clowns, Legos, stuffed
miniature bears, strewn across my frontal lobe.
Maybe they'll find questions on my little brain trees:
what's for dinner, why can't someone teach me
how to work DirecTV? When will I see you again?
Manny is kind. He tells me how long each pounding session
will last—only two minutes he says into the microphone.
How's it going? Fine, I say, but I'd prefer to think about a kiss
I'll have in the future, after they scrape the walls of my brain,
eliminate extra synapses, remove connections no longer needed.
That's the key, I think, as the banging becomes unbearable,
and the boy from camp who couldn't kiss appears next to me
begging for another chance.

ABANDONED

They were in the gutter
a pair of man-sized
flip flops, fat toe prints embedded
in the rubber, not really old
still looked in decent shape
but some man kicked them off
discarded them, left them
to get rolled over by a stroller
run over by a Toyota or bus load
of children eating Cheez-Its
texting pictures of naked body parts
final assault to a pair of innocent flip
flops. Who would do such a thing?
What kind of man
wears flip flops
tosses them into the street
when he no longer wants them?
Is he the kind of man you'd respect?
Want? Could you love this man?
I do. I love him for walking barefoot
down Genessee, the heat of asphalt
searing his calloused feet. I love him
for wanting to be free of silly shoes
that offer no support, no elegance, shoes
to put on in a hurry, without thought
shoes that make a slapping smacking sound
shoes you want to happily abandon knowing
a stranger is likely to step on them
crush their uselessness.
I love him for ending it.

DOING NOTHING

I lie down on my bed, pretend to read
On the Road, the book I always lie about
having read. I stare out the window
think about the day Miss Josephs,
my fifth grade teacher, shared my book report
on *The Red Pony* with the class:
an example of really excellent work!
But today I'm doing nothing, just staring
at my fingernails. I choose to believe
the latest research, that doing nothing can lead
to bursts of creativity, ideas flowing
like a revitalized creek through a ghost town.
Lava can erupt from an inactive volcano.
I get up from the bed and sit on the floor
in a half spinal twist, apologize to the dead,
which takes a few hours since many people I love
have recently died. *I'm sorry I didn't come over sooner,*
I tell my mother; *sorry, Dad, I made fun of you
when you said things like "he's as old as the hills."*
I'm sorry to a poet who loved me.
To be precise, and completely fair to myself,
the word "doing" in front of the word "nothing" changes
the word nothing—lifts it into the world of action.
I realize this as I stare at the electrical outlet,
wonder what I should plug into it,
what kind of lamp might work well in that corner.
Maybe one of those tall skinny metal poles,
three bulbs shooting straight up—
something to illuminate the ceiling, but no,

it'll look cheap, out of style, and anyway,
maybe I should keep one part of the room dark,
so ideas might grow like mushrooms, populate
my brain with plans I won't pursue.
It might be time to *really* read *On the Road*,
but another's stream of consciousness
competing with my own might incite an inertia tsunami.
I'm sorry to the dogs I loved but never cleaned up after.
I'm sorry for all the time I wasted as a child,
when doing nothing was all they expected of the girl
with the chalkboard and dolls.

A FLY WITH ONE WING IS WATCHING ME

I remember this fly from long ago
when it had two wings. I was living
in Boston, tried to kill it so many hot
summer nights, terrorized me as I
tried to sleep, circling the chaos
in my head, knew him so well
I called him Jack, tried to make it
a fun thing, this fly intent on ruining
my life. Now he's in LA, languishing
on the soft chair across the room,
watching me work. I can see he's less
a fly since he's lost a wing, and I want
to know his anguish. *Come here little fly*,
I gently call to him, but flies are so
nervous they think we're all trying
to kill them so they don't wait to hear
what we have to say. I approach him
slowly, put my finger out, invite him
to hop on but he doesn't move. Maybe
his one wing is too tired to lift, so I sit
next to him, remind him of his glory
days back when he could torment me
how much fun it must have been for him.
He doesn't move. I consider flicking him
across the room or smashing him
right there, but why? It's clear he came by
to see me, find out how I'm doing,
acknowledge the past when his buzz
was his life and he couldn't resist
being the best fly he could be.

THE LIVES THEY LIVED

I study the dead. What drove
that woman out of the farmhouse,
why did he kill his lover, how did she lose
her mind, what made him fly so many missions?

I will be dead one day. No more roses
to forget to smell, no need to know
the outside temperature, wait for the coffee to drip.
What will people remember?
What might they say?

"She kept a hidden locker filled with typewriters—
Royals, Adlers, Remingtons, Olympias . . ."
"She ordered birthday presents for her youngest child
two days before she died." "She was just a nurse."
"After her missionary husband died, she went to live with his killers."

CANDLELIGHT ASYLUM

Do not enter my candlelight asylum
where we dance in our terry cloth robes,
hair pinned up like discarded Barbies,
our feet crushed in pink ballet slippers.
I lied.
There is no one here.
I am all alone, just me
in my grown up sled bed, comforter
around my feet, head propped with flat pillows,
no cases, yellow around the edges,
a furnace coughing up wet music.
This is no place for someone so alive, juicy
abundantly humane,
so soft in her silk underwear.
You may enter, but
only you, you with the smile and dark hair,
you with the stride, the hands.
You look like you could get me
out, and I trust that you will.
Come on in.
No one here but me
and the candles, though they're burning fast,
room darkening as the breeze pours through the windows.
I don't even know your name or where you're from.
Please take my slippers.
No one is listening
my inside voice, my inside words, no one hears—
not even the handsome nurse
who brings my tray of kisses.

Oh I lied again, there is no nurse.
Don't believe a word I tell you, but please
take me away.
Do I have to wait for disaster before someone
plucks me
like the wilted daisy in the jar by the window,
places me in clear water in a silver vase? Hurry
before sunset goes bad. Join me
on the last train to the missing planet.

COMFORT

I am not through
the looking glass
but stuck inside
like a bite
of turkey
lodged
in a crowded
esophagus.
I watch others slide down
see them scatter at the bottom
wild headdresses ancient
fears, they flame the fires
while I hold my matches
tight in my fist
live upside down
walk on the clouds
look up at the sea
its waves breaking
above me
And when I pray
I don't look up or down
but to the side, because God
is on my shoulder
telling a joke
I've already heard
but there's comfort
always knowing
the punch line.

YOU'VE LOVED TOO MANY GEMINIS,

the psychic tells me
can't trust a word they say
they're evil twins who live
to get their way.
I'm watching her mouth,
her lipstick smeared
above the lip line.
You're wrong, I tell her,
I've only loved one Gemini,
what kind of psychic are you?
I *feel* it, she says, I see Geminis
floating around you
heating up the air you breathe
permeating every cell,
I can smell them all over you,
a halo of twins pulling you apart.
Look, I tell her, you're a fake psychic,
a psychic who needs her eyes
checked, and then I left to visit
someone else who thinks
he knows the real me.

COMING CLEAN

I've never read Jane Austen
I don't know how to swim
My gravy's not made from scratch
I toss glass bottles in the blue bin

I have removed my clothes for strangers
I have more than five drinks per week
The exotic fish in my tank are not exotic
I stole a rare shell from a protected reef

I once served a hamburger from the floor
I habitually curse
I have no upper body strength
I stole change from my mother's purse

I poked holes in my dolls' mouths
I really want to believe
How these burdens have weighed me down:
Kisses I'm still waiting to receive

"YOU MUST BE JOKING, I NEVER EAT BREAKFAST,"

said Michael Caine in *Get Carter*,
chest bare, lighting up in bed,
a cold-blooded killer, the morning after
a one night stand, a "roll in the hay"
as my mother's friend used to say.
I wanted to be that woman lying
next to him under the covers
black mascara streaked down my cheeks,
wild hair, our legs entwined, seconds away
from the men with guns breaking down the door.
Why do we like these tough guys?
Million dollar question for the Million Dollar
Movie which I'd watch every Saturday night
on the little black & white when my parents
were asleep. *Love with the Proper Stranger*,
Natalie Wood gets pregnant by Steve McQueen,
he marries her, does the "right thing," and at fourteen
I fantasized about going too far in an old Corvette
somewhere in Brooklyn or Queens with a guy
who looked like Steve McQueen.
My mother was relieved we lived in Manhattan,
no cars for her to worry about, no tunnels or bridges,
no back seats, just the Broadway Bus where nothing much
can happen except you might see someone get on
with a bullet hole in his shoulder like I did going home
from 57th Street after a "date" with a boy I didn't know.
We went to see *Prudence and the Pill*, I was embarrassed,
he was unappealing, and then on the bus a man with blood
dripping from underneath his coat. I used to wonder

what a "roll in the hay" might be like with a murderer.
Would he tell me he never ate breakfast, would he tell me
why he killed? Michael Caine went after the men
who murdered his brother. Makes sense, I guess. Revenge
is popular. If someone set fire to my house, I would find them.
I would borrow a gun. Everyone, it seems, has one.
I would pull the trigger on an empty stomach. I never
eat breakfast either.

FISH'S LAMENT

The deep sea diver in the video:
wetsuit, fins, tank on his back,
reaches out to pet an Atlantic

Bluefin Tuna, and I wonder
does this fish want to be touched?
But the fish swims right into this diver's

hands, wanting more.
I doubt this fish has ever
been caressed like this.

I would swim a lifetime,
the fish tells his friends,
to ever feel that good again.

Kim (Freilich) Dower has published five acclaimed collections of poetry and was City Poet Laureate of West Hollywood from October 2016 to October 2018. Her most recent book, the bestselling *I Wore This Dress Today for You, Mom*, an Eric Hoffer Book Award finalist, was called a "fantastic collection" by the *Washington Post*, "impressively insightful, thought-provoking, and truly memorable" by the *Midwest Book Review*, and Shelf-Awareness said, "These gorgeous gems are energized by the sheer power of her wit and irreverent style." *Air Kissing on Mars*, Kim's first collection, was described by the *Los Angeles Times* as "sensual and evocative . . . seamlessly combining humor and heartache." *Slice of Moon* was called "unexpected and sublime" by *O* magazine; *Last Train to the Missing Planet* was described as "poems that speak about the grey space between tragedy and tenderness, memory and loss, fragility and perseverance" by Richard Blanco; and *Sunbathing on Tyrone Power's Grave* won the 2020 Independent Publishers Book Awards Gold Medal for Poetry. Kim's work has been featured in numerous literary journals, including *Plume, Ploughshares, Rattle, James Dickey Review*, and Garrison Keillor's *The Writer's Almanac*, and her poems are included in several anthologies, notably, *Wide Awake: Poets of Los Angeles and Beyond*. She teaches poetry workshops for Antioch University, UCLA Extension Writers' Program, and the West Hollywood Library. Born and raised on the Upper West Side of New York City and a graduate of Emerson College in Boston, Kim is also the proud owner of Kim-from-L.A., a long-standing literary publicity company that helps authors around the country get the word out about their wonderful books. To learn more about Kim, visit her website: www.kimdowerpoetry.com